The Shroud

Opa

With revilement and torture let us put him to the test
That we may have proof of his gentleness and try his patience.
Let us condemn him to a shameful death,
For according to his own words, God will take care of him.

Wisdom 2:12

Liebe mensch gmbh, Wien 4/12/2017

Table of Contents

Preface 4
Provenance 9
Historical references prior to 1350 18
The Cloth 23
Carbon Dating 30
A painting? 36
The times of Jesus 43
Image evidence on the cloth 49
Burial 64
Clues from Art 70
Probabilities 76

Preface

In the late fall of 1947, I had recently been discharged from the Navy and was enrolled in Manhattan College under the GI-Bill. I had just turned twenty. My dad wrote me to say that his friend Dr. Anthony Sava was giving a lecture at the New York Explorer's Club on something called *The Shroud of Turin,* and that I was invited….and so I went. It was so intriguing, that for the subsequent sixty five years I've read and studied every book I could get a hold of, weighing the latest evidence as to the likelihood that the image on the Shroud is that of the historical man Jesus from Nazareth.

The Shroud is a long narrow strip *(14' by 3.5')* of linen cloth with a very faint negative front and back image of a naked man who had been scourged, apparently crucified, stabbed in the ribs and had his scalp bloodied. **It is the most analyzed and debated archeological artifact in human history!** Well over 2,000 books and papers have been written about it.

On the following page can be seen this Shroud. The eight pairs of triangular disfiguration marks are where the folded cloth was burned in a fire in 1532 and patched, and the two vertical parallel dark lines are fold lines. The four very dark splotches are scorched areas.

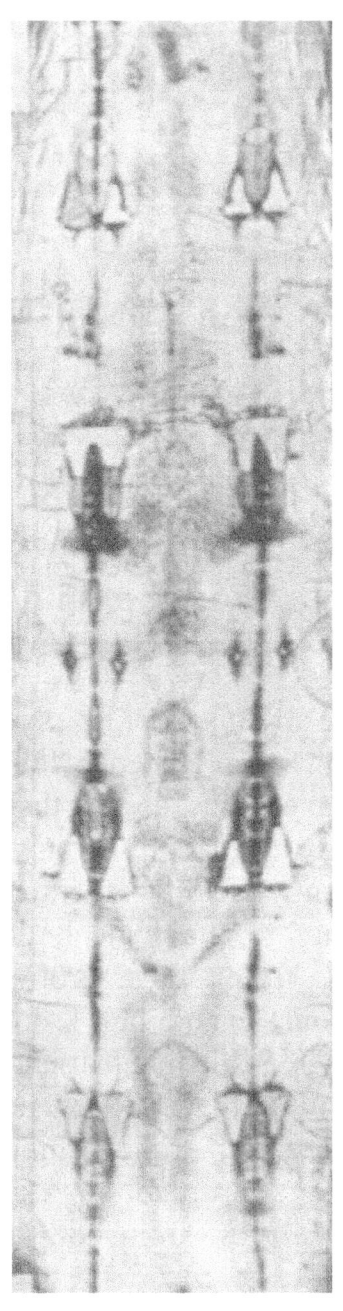

The purpose of this booklet is to summarize for you grandchildren, the evidence both positive and negative, that I have come across that I believe to be reasonable. I have culled out anything emotional, ridiculous, anything smacking of miracles and the like. I've limited it only to the logical, clear-cut evidence whether scientific, from art or from history. I tread lightly on myth and legend but I don't ignore them. Remember, Heinrich Schliemann found the ancient city of Troy by believing that the legend from Homer's *Odyssey* had a trace of truth behind it, and Israeli archeologists have made a number of similar discoveries based on biblical *'stories'* from both the Old and New Testaments.

So, as I present all of what I consider the reliable, reasonable evidence, I want you to make believe you are an archeologist, and try not to let your religious beliefs influence your reasoning. Weigh the evidence the same as you would if you were studying the authenticity of a relic of Pharaoh Ramses II or Tutankhamen. Just use your common sense, and only at the end of this booklet decide whether the image in the Shroud is in all probability that of a historical Jew who was executed by the Romans sometime around 30 AD in Jerusalem, or is it an unbelievably brilliant 14th century fake.

In 1902, the famous Professor of Anatomy at the Sorbonne Yves Delage, **a professed atheist**, reported to the French Academy that in his opinion the Shroud probably was that of Jesus. This caused such furor in France that he later wrote:

"If instead of Christ, there were a question of some historical person like Sargon, or Achilles, or one of the Pharaohs, no one would have thought of making any objection....I recognize Christ as a historical personage, and I see no reason why anyone should be scandalized that there still might exist material traces of his earthly life."

****

All the bits and pieces of Shroud evidence are like a jumble of jigsaw parts with some of the pieces still missing. As we go through this book, little by little pieces here and there will begin fitting together. In the end, we'll have connected enough of the dots to begin seeing the true picture. By then most of you will have come to your conclusion as to whether the face on this most sacred relic in Christendom, is some sort of photographic/chemical image of the dead Jesus of Nazareth.

One final word. There might be a minor point or a date here or there that I've not got completely right, but overall, the evidence is how I gleaned it from my studies.

So here we go!

Chapter 1

Provenance

When buying a work of art, before paying a lot of money for possibly a forgery, the judicious buyer asks for its *provenance* i.e. the known thoroughly documented historic origin or history of the work. For example, I recently saw a PBS show on Leonardo daVinci and in it, they discussed a recently discovered work believed to be his. Its provenance only dates back a century or so, but the other bits and pieces of evidence have lead most experts to conclude it to be authentic. In this Chapter-1, I present the actual well documented history of the Shroud. In Chapter-2, I'll review historical evidence of the earlier existence of a cloth that could most likely be the Shroud.

Provenance:
1357 AD The Shroud that we know exists in Turin today, was attracting large crowds of pilgrims, so much so that souvenir medallions were sold. The relic belonged to Jeanne de Vergy, the widow of a much-honored Knight Geoffrey de Charny-1, who died the year before fighting the English at the battle of Poitiers. The widow lived in Lirey in northeastern France. Geoffrey supposedly arranged *"....to have the said cloth placed in the said church* (Blessed Mary at Lirey) *that by renewal of pilgrimage the church might be enriched with the*

offerings made by the faithful...." She and her family refused to divulge how they acquired it.

(Shroud souvenir medallion from the 1350s. Note the front and back body images)

1389 Bishop Pierre de'Arcis of Troyes *(who wrote the quote at the bottom of the previous page)* apparently out of jealousy or greed, continued his above letter to the Pope claiming the shroud to be nothing more than a **painting,** and what's more, he knew who the artist was! The Bishop then attempted to ban its exhibition, but was overridden by higher church authorities.

1453 The widow's daughter Margaret de Baufremont decided to give the Shroud to the Duke of Savoy for safer keeping *(from the Hundred Years War)* at his castle at Chambrey in southeastern France. There it was kept in the chapel folded up in a silver reliquary.

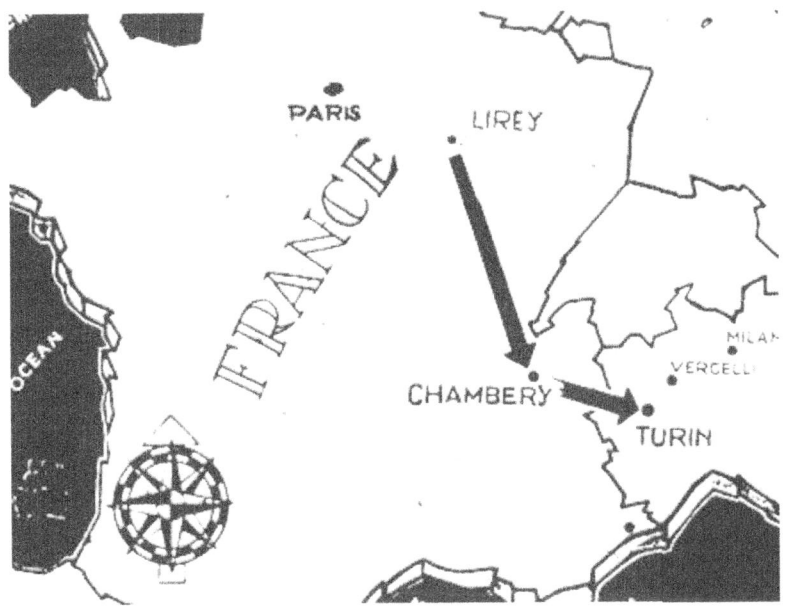

1532 The church at Chambrey burned down but the silver reliquary was rescued after one corner and an edge had melted away, in the process burning those portions of the Shroud's folds *(see pages 5 and 12)*.

Nuns subsequently cut out the sixteen major burned areas and sewed in *'14th Century'* linen patches.

Below see where the folds were burned.

On the following page, see the grey triangles. They are where nuns sewed in patches after the fire. The very central roughly circular areas down the centerline around chest and knees, are water stains. The straight horizontal and vertical dotted lines are how it was folded.

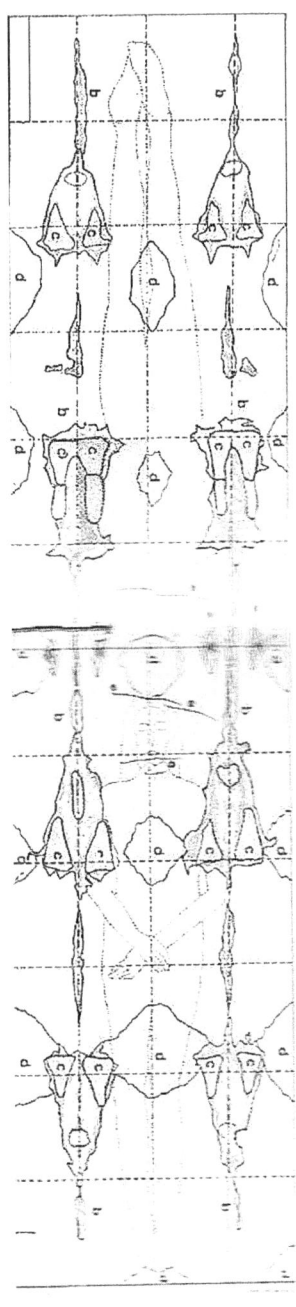

1578 The Duke of Savoy transferred custodianship of the shroud to the Cathedral in Turin.

1500-1900 Periodically over these years for important religious and royal events, the Shroud was put on public outdoor exposition

(On exposition. Note all the hands holding its edge)

(Exhibition of the Shroud in Turin in the early 1900s)

1898 The Shroud was photographed for the first time. Remember that the image on the Shroud *(except for the blood)* is a negative one. Also, remember that cameras in those days produced negative images. The camera's result was then a negative of a negative. In other words, the 1898 film came out as a positive! Thus, for the first time in the Shroud's history, a clear visible figure of a dead man and particularly his haunting face, was revealed.

From that moment on, instead of being a little known local relic, the Shroud suddenly became of interest across the Christian world. Doctors *(such as Anthony Sava who gave the lecture I attended in 1947)* and a wide variety of scientists and experts from different disciplines and religious beliefs, then began learning things about the Shroud, and crucifixion hitherto unknown since Roman times.

1931 Shroud was re-photographed with more modern equipment. *All the actual Shroud pictures in this book come from these 1931 photos which I wrote away for sixty some odd years ago.*

1978 A team of enthusiastic American scientists including NASA experts, came to Turin and received permission to do the first forensic study of the cloth.

1983 The House of Savoy transferred ownership of the Shroud to the Catholic Church *(i.e. The Vatican).*

1988 Three reputable scientific labs obtained a tiny sample of the cloth, and all three, carbon dated the cloth to the 1300s! As scientists tend to do, they superciliously proclaimed the Shroud to be an **unquestionable** religious fake! Since I had worked at the Atomic scientific labs at Oak Ridge, I assumed the scientists to be correct, and despite the vast amount of contrary evidence, that the Shroud therefore had to be some kind of amazing forgery. I was devastated as were thousands of believers in its authenticity.

1990s Additional information came to light concerning how carbon dating can produce inaccurate results if the sample tested is contaminated, or inadvertently not taken from the original material. I again became a firm believer!

Chapter 2

Historical references prior to 1350

In this chapter, we review some of the various references in history, art, literature and coins, possibly related to images in cloth of the face and/or figure.

April, 30 AD-A commonly accepted date of Jesus' death under Pilate *(procurator from 26-36 AD)*. The linen burial cloth<u>s</u> *(plural)* are reported in the gospels as found folded in the empty tomb.

50 AD-Tradition and Bishop Eusebius *(263-339)* has Thaddeus *(the apostle Jude)* bringing an <u>image-bearing</u> sacred cloth to ill King Abgar V of Eddessa *(an ancient city in what is now central Turkey)*. This image-bearing cloth was known as the *Mandylion*. The tradition must've been fairly widespread because in 954 the monks of St. Catherine's Monastery at the base of Mt. Sinai painted the below picture of the traditional incident!

(King Abgar receiving the Mandylion from St. Jude)

90± Somewhere around this time, the Christians in Edessa underwent a severe Roman persecution and there are no further references to the so-called *Mandylion*.

192- Edessa was once again Christian.

525- While rebuilding Edessa's western city gate the *Mandylion* was found hidden away in the wall. A hymn written at that period notes the beauty of the **holy image** on the *Tetradiplon (double folded in four)* cloth.

629- Emperor Justinian minted a coin with the image of Jesus' face on it, supposedly taken from the *Mandylion*. Note the uncanny resemblance to the Shroud?

From about that time onward until this very day, all pictures of Christ look like this i.e. long parted hair, beard and mustache. Prior to that time all images of Jesus presented him as looking Roman i.e. short hair and beardless! *(see pages 70 and 71)*

638- The Muslims conquered Edessa and renamed it Urfa.

944- Byzantine Emperor Romanus Lacapenus[1] marched his army to Edessa and threatened the Muslims to either give him the *Mandylion*, or be attacked. He received it and installed it in Constantinople.

1130- Pope Stephen II described the *Mandylion* in Constantinople as bearing, *"...the glorious features of Jesus' face and the majestic form **of his entire body.**"* Does that sound like our Shroud?

1144- Muslims ruthlessly obliterated all traces of Christianity from Edessa.

1201- Nicholas Mesarites the keeper of the Emperor's relics in Constantinople, listed among them, *"....the burial shrouds of Christ: These are of linen. They are of cheap and easy to find materials still smelling of myrrh and defying decay since they wrapped the **outlineless**, fragrant-with-myrrh, **naked body** after the Passion......"*

1204- The *'devout, noble'* crusaders *(primarily French)* of the 4th Crusade, sacked, raped and pillaged the

---

[1] I'm sorry, but that was the man's name!

Christian city of Constantinople, looting and carrying off whatever pleased them. A few months earlier, one of these crusaders Frenchman Robert de Clari, wrote of having admired the *Mandylion* which was displayed in the Church of St. Mary at Blachernae.

"*....it was stretched upright each Friday so that one could clearly see the **figure** of the Lord, but neither Greek nor Frank knows what became of the cloth after the city was taken (sacked).*" Sound like our Shroud?

1314- King Philippe *'the Fair'* of France was in need of funds. Looking around he saw that the wealthiest source was the Knights Templar, a military/monastic **crusader** organization *(Templars took the vows of poverty, chastity and obedience, and were legendary in their bravery in battle against the infidels).*

Philippe had Templar leader Grand Master Jacques de Molay arrested on the trumped up charge of heresy for *'worshiping'* a mysterious **holy face on a cloth.** Molay was then burned at the stake. Thus did this 'virtuous' monarch acquire the Templars possessions. However, the alleged cloth with the mysterious face on it, was never found. Burned at the stake along with de Molay was a companion knight interestingly enough named **Geoffrey de Charny**.

Was this cloth the *Mandylion* which vanished when the French looted Constantinople? Was this the Shroud put on exposition in 1357 by the widow of a later knight also by the name of **Geoffrey de Charny**? It is certainly a reasonable possibility.

Chapter 3

The Cloth

As noted earlier, the Shroud is a long narrow *(14' by 3.5')* strip of well-made linen on which are the faint negative images of a man, both back and front views. Note that one can only see the image if one stands several feet away. The image is similar looking to the scorch marks one gets when ironing a white shirt with too hot an iron. As will be made clear in a later chapter, the image is of a real man, **not a painting!** Also on the cloth are blood stains which are positive *(dark)*. There are also eight pairs of large triangular patches and burned areas, and some water marks from the fire in 1532 mentioned back on pages 12-13.

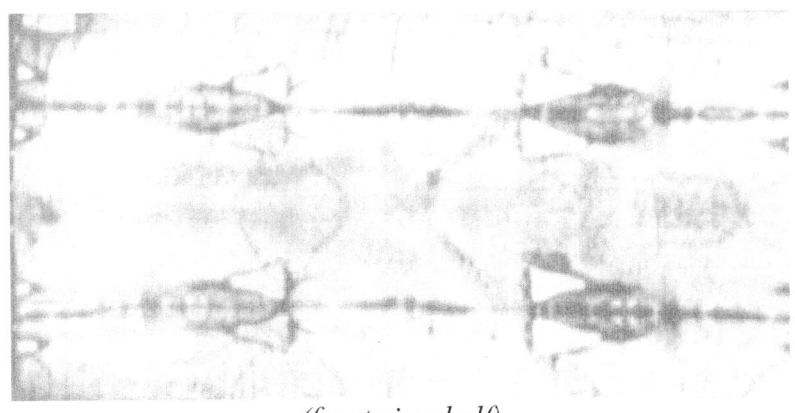

(front view half)

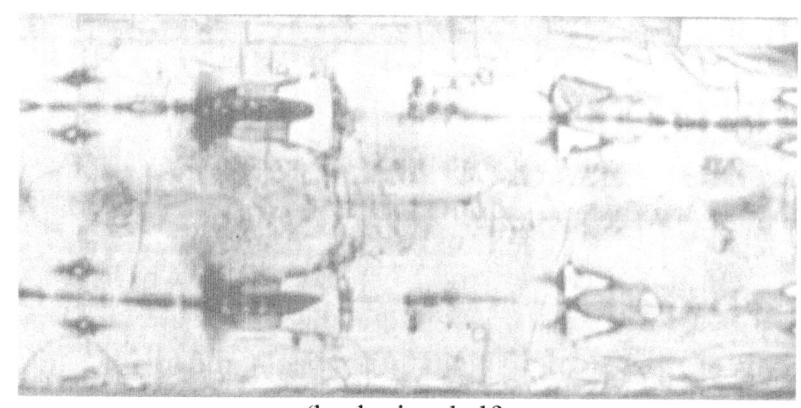
(back view half)

According to textile experts, the weave is herringbone twill, a weave common at the time of Christ but on the other hand rather uncommon in medieval Europe. However, it must be noted that though the weave can be found in ancient wool and silk, there seem to be no museum examples in linen.

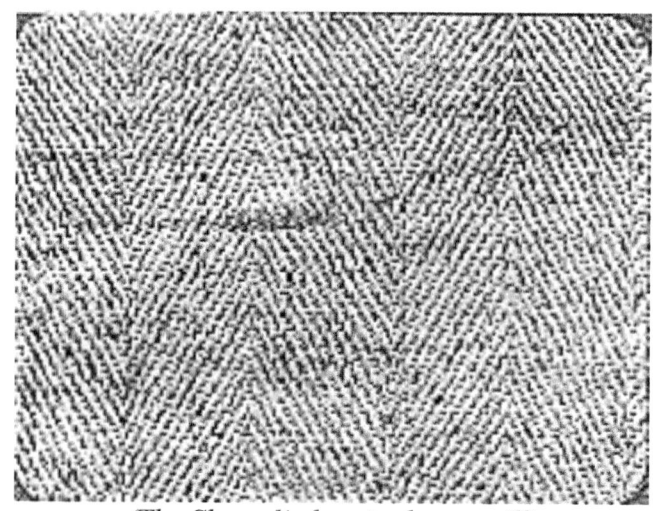
(The Shroud's herringbone twill)

To weave such a large, odd shaped cloth by hand must've taken a significant trouble and expense. So why would a forger go to all the bother of choosing a weave most everyone in 13th Century France was unfamiliar with? Why not simply use a normal' weave? If someone in the 1300s wanted to fool the gullible, illiterate, superstitious people, any used cheap bed sheet would have done the job without the slightest question. Why go to all the trouble of making or finding an odd shaped linen of Middle East weave?

<u>Limestone dust evidence in the cloth:</u>
Found in the cloth by the forensic specialists were limestone dust particles. Limestone comes from various sea creatures that died millions of years ago and accumulated on various world seafloors. The chemical makeup of limestone therefore depends on what type of creatures they were at the time. The limestone of France for example differs in chemical makeup from the limestone of Colorado or China. So, guess what? When the Fermi Lab in Chicago ran a spectrographic analysis of the Shroud dust it was almost an almost **identical match** for the limestone found around Jerusalem....not of France!

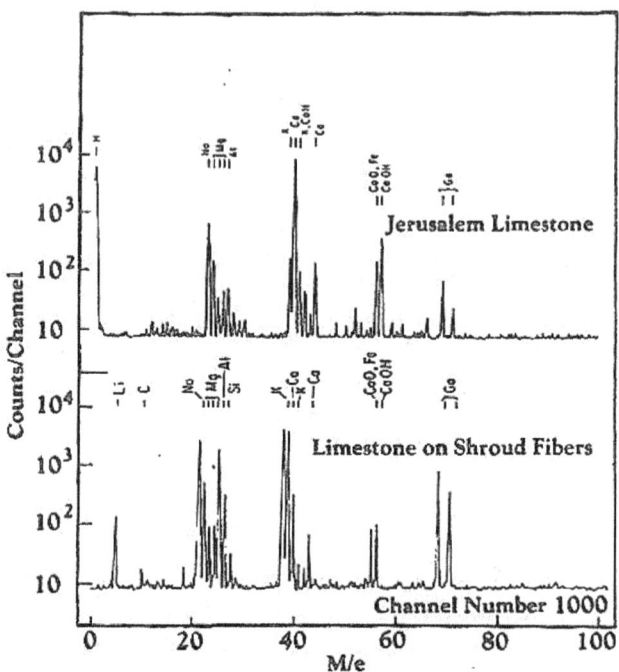

Pollen spores evidence in the cloth:

The Shroud was examined by botanist experts for spores. Bearing in mind that for centuries, the Shroud was periodically exposed in the open air to crowds, it is not at all surprising that the pollen and spores of European plants were found in abundance. What was more interesting though, was that spores of salt-loving plants such as from around the Dead Sea were also found as well as those common to Central Turkey *(where Edessa once was)!* Of course the doubters explain that these spores could've blown all the way from the Middle East, across the Mediterranean to France! It's of course possible, but let's face it, a bit hard to swallow!

150 years earlier evidence:

In the museum in Budapest is a famous illuminated religious text called the ***Pray Manuscript***, written and beautifully illustrated by monks in **1192-93** i.e. before Constantinople was sacked and **150 years before the carbon dating date!** One stylized art scene depicts Jesus being laid in a shroud. What is significant about it?:

1. The body is laid out exactly as in the Shroud, naked with crossed hands.
2. Only 4 fingers, no thumbs are shown as in the Shroud! *(What sensible artist would leave out the thumbs?)*

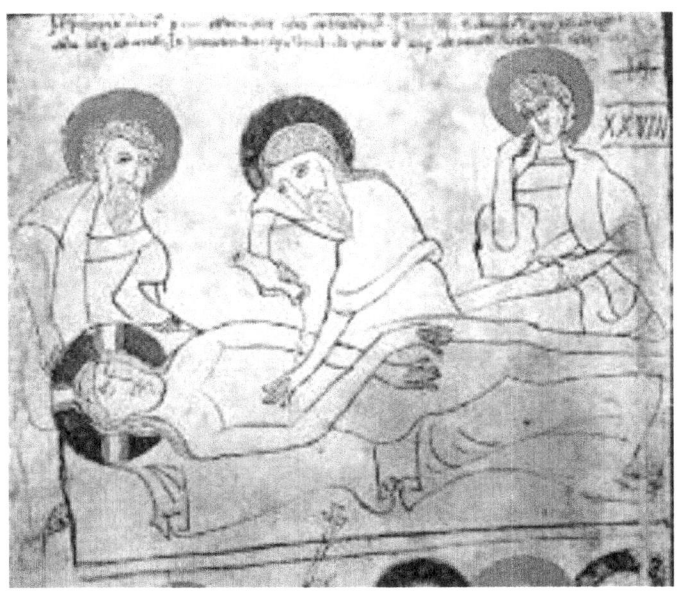

3. The cloth shows what looks like a herringbone twill!

4- And most significant of all, the Shroud has seven unexplained, what look like tiny burn holes referred to as the *poker holes*

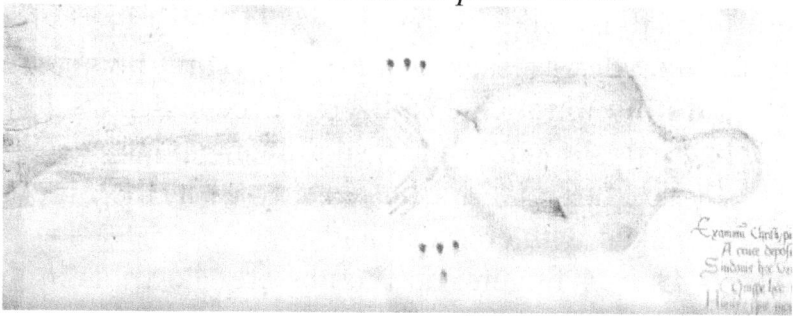

*(1516 Shroud drawing **before** the 1532 fire. Note the seven so-called 'poker holes'*

Guess what?! The Pray Manuscript oddly enough also has seven pointless holes depicted in the twill!

Did the forgers in France go to the ridiculous trouble of going to Budapest to copy an obscure *(at least to a Frenchmen)* Hungarian document? **or,**

did the Hungarian Monks copy from the Shroud....**back in 1192-3!?**

Evidence based on medieval burials:

Medieval shrouds were generally in the shape of a bed sheet, not a long narrow 14' by 4' strip of cloth. The forger would've had to go to the time and expense of having such an odd shaped linen woven! Why, when any purchaser of the fake relic would expect a shroud like those used at that time? Also in the Shroud, the man's head is at the closed end, and his feet at the open end *(see picture on page 6)*. This is the reverse of medieval Europe where the body is like how you pull the sheet up after you get into bed. Why would a 1300s forger put the head where the French expected the feet to be? How would the forger know that was the way ancient Jews wrapped their dead?

Chapter 4

Carbon Dating

In 1988, three very reputable atomic labs were given a tiny sample ***from the edge*** of the Shroud to carbon date. The results shocked the believers of the authenticity of the Shroud such as me! All three labs came up with an origin date of around 1300! The scientists' conclusion seemed to be a supercilious *"Ignore all other evidence, the Shroud is obviously a fake. The chance of us scientists being wrong is like one in a trillion!"* after all in this modern day and age science trumps the ridiculous superstitions of God and religion. I was devastated. I worked at the atomic scientific labs at Oak Ridge. The labs couldn't be wrong. And, after all, they all came up with the same answer!

About here, you must be asking yourself, *"What the heck is carbon dating?"* So, I'll take a moment to explain:

Carbon makes up that black stuff when you burn toast, or a piece of wood. There are basically two kinds of carbon atoms floating around the earth's atmosphere: **Carbon-14** *(radioactive)* atoms and **Carbon-12** *(stable/normal)* atoms. Radioactive atoms give off radiation which means over time, they *'decay'* into some other element. Stable atoms don't give off/lose anything, and therefore over millions of years never change i.e. remain carbon. In the air we are breathing, let's for the sake of simplicity assume the ratio of Carbon-14 atoms to Carbon-12 atoms is say something like **12 to 9988**!

Just about every living thing has carbon in it, be it bacterium, a blade of grass or an elephant. Now the minute the living thing dies, it ceases to breathe or eat or absorb any more fresh carbon. After death, the C-14 atoms give off radiation such that after every 5000+ years half of it decays and becomes some other element.

For example let's say we pluck a living blade of grass containing 10,000 carbon atoms

12 would be C-14 and the remaining
9,988 would be C-12.
10,000 total atoms of carbon

Now 5000 years later, there would be:
6 C-14s (the other 6 having given off radiation and disappeared)
9,988 would still be C-12s
9,994 total atoms of carbon

Now 5,000 more years later there would be:
3 C-14s (the other 3 having disappeared)
9,988 would still be C-12s
9,991 total atoms of carbon

So you see, by counting how much C-14 is still remaining compared to the C-12, scientists can approximate how long ago our blade of grass ceased absorbing carbon i.e. died.

****

Getting back to the Shroud. After 1988, people began realizing that though carbon dating is correct, the answer can be quite misleading depending on the state of the sample that was used.

Example:
Unrelated to the Shroud business, Dr. Rosalie David of the Manchester Egyptian Museum sent mummy tissue **and** a bit of the linen wrapping it, to be carbon dated and there was a difference between the mummy and its wrapping, the **linen being 1,000 years 'younger'!** The scientists concluded that the reason must've been because someone had re-wrapped the mummy a 1,000 years later. Dr. David didn't buy that explanation, so she sent an Ibis mummy and its wrapping since nobody would've wasted time rewrapping a bird. The results were similar with a 600 year error, the wrapping again being younger!

No one could explain for certain, the reasons for the above discrepancies other than the cloth samples had been different/altered in some way. Perhaps after burial the samples had later been contaminated by organic residue from some later living, fungi, bacteria or perhaps beeswax smoke of some kind.

With respect to the Shroud sample, it turns out that there are several possible explanations.

1) Over the centuries there were multiple expositions, all with candles and their bee's wax drippings and smoke. There was also incense smoke.
2) The sample was taken along the very edge. My coats, sweaters, trousers etc. all acquire frayed edges over time. *(your Oma then much to my dismay would then throw them into the garbage)* Even more so the Shroud must've frayed from being held up by its edge so often. Over the centuries, the frayed edges of such a precious relic would most likely have been devotedly repaired, **of course using 'new' thread.**
3) This past winter there was a lot of flu. So we were told to avoid touching hands at Mass and in public, and to frequently wash our hands to avoid spreading bacteria. What about the bacteria over the centuries of all those unwashed hands[2] that held the edge? *(see the painting below and on page 14. Look at the 16 hands all holding the edge of the Shroud).*

---

[2] Your second cousin Lucy Cotter age eleven, just completed a science project. In it she grew measurable cultures grown from the bacteria on the hands of her brothers and sister, both before and after scrubbing!

(Look at all the dirty hands holding the edge)

4) Dr. Garza-Valdes finding a *'bioplastic'* clear acrylic-like covering on the sample's threads similar to the insulation on an electric wire. This apparently the result of centuries of carbon bearing fungi growth and was also found on Dr. David's ibis mummy linen.

So the result of all the above is that the labs' dates were correct, <u>**for the sample sent them**</u>. This does not necessarily mean the sample was uncontaminated over the centuries by fungi growth or other matter like repair thread, bee's wax, smoke, bacteria etc. As author Ian Wilson sarcastically commented in *'The Blood and the Shroud'*,

"*So clearly no one should as yet regard all this as having proven Garza-Valdes's argument for how the Shroud dating may have been so seriously skewed. None the less, might one be forgiven for suggesting that the radiocarbon laboratories' so confident odds of 'one in a thousand trillion' against their being wrong are beginning to look just a little overstated!"*

In other words, the 1988 carbon dating no longer should be accepted as being *conclusive proof* that the Shroud originated somewhere in the 1300s. Therefore, until the laboratories can demonstrate with mummies and their wrappings that they can properly decontaminate the linen samples, **all the plethora of other Shroud evidence is still in play!**

Chapter 5

A painting?

You may remember from earlier, that in 1389 the local bishop claimed the Shroud to be fake; a painting. Other skeptics claim it to be some form of painting, or possibly a medieval form of **photo**! or the result of laying a cloth over a hot bloody statue.

The purpose of this chapter, is to point out how unlike the carbon dating, the idea of a painting is ridiculous.

1. All the coloring of the image on the Shroud is limited to only the very surface fibrils. If it were any sort of painting, the coloring would have soaked down into the cloth at least a thread deep.
2. A medieval artist would never *'make mistakes'* like leaving off the thumbs, or showing Jesus nailed through the wrists rather than the palms as every other painting in the last 1,000 years has shown. And no one would ever have been so vulgar as to depict Jesus as naked! *(see page 63 of Israeli archeologists' depiction of a crucifixion)*.
3. French artists of the 14th Century were far from highly knowledgeable concerning anatomy and the proportions of the human body. The Shroud body however is perfectly proportioned. If

some genius painter did this, then who was he? Where are his other works?

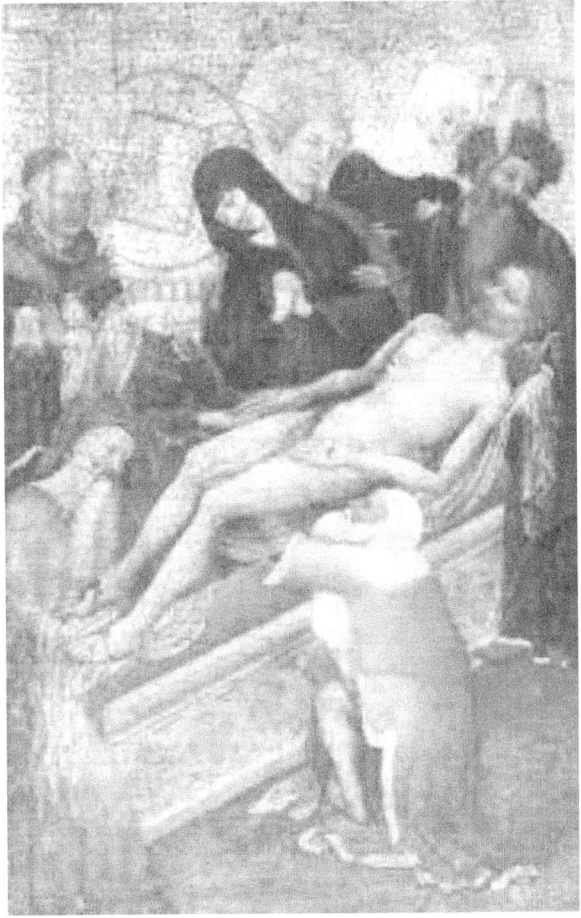

(Medieval French art, note poor proportions)

4- Most telling of all however is that no artist prior to photography, **has ever** been able to paint an accurate negative, for the simple reason that he would need a camera negative of his negative *(which would be a positive)* to verify whether or not he had painted the original negative correctly. Anyone who has ever looked at old family negatives, knows that it is difficult to know whom the negative is of. If I showed the below negative, nobody would gamble a $100 that it was John Wayne. But the positive is 100% clear.

Below are two attempts by medieval French artists at copying the Shroud image. Immediately below them are the results of letting my computer turn their drawings into positives.

(Artist's attempt at a negative)

(Turned positive by my computer)

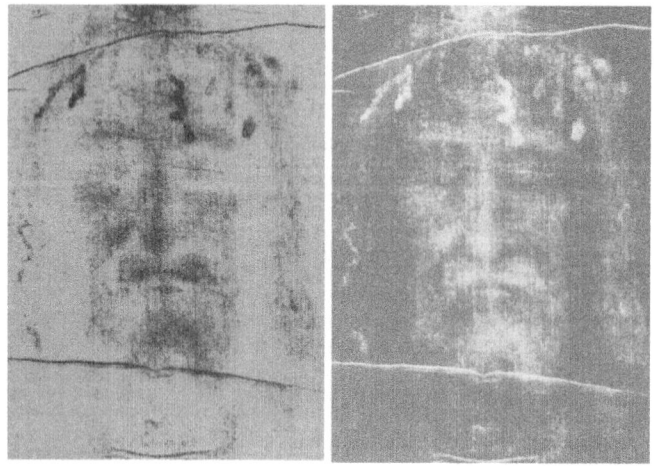

(Original 1931 negative vs photo positive)

The results are ridiculous! Clearly our unknown genius forger in1350± was never able to check his negative work. He had to wait 600 years for the advent of photography when in 1898 the world first saw the positive of the Shroud. So tell me then, how he could possibly have gotten it exactly right?

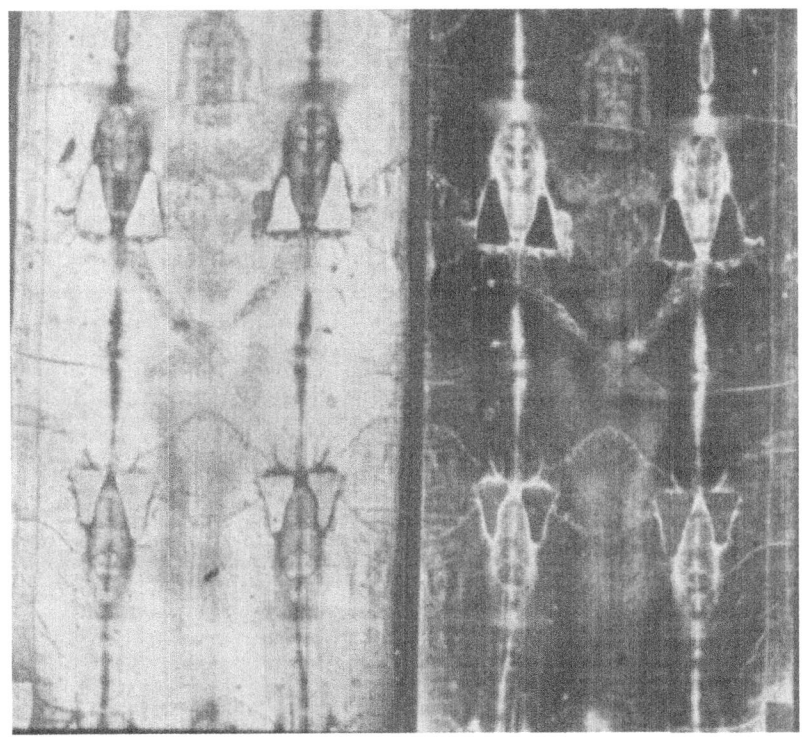

Original 1931 negative vs positive (the front half only)

Lastly the Pasadena Jet Propulsion Lab developed a *3D Image Analyzer*. It was for creating 3D images of the surface of the Moon and Mars from space photos in order to determine the height of the terrain. When applied to any painting, the result is always a flat distortion, never 3D! The same for photographs taken of Lab Employee's faces. **But when applied to the face on the Shroud, out sprung the man's face!**

(The 3D face from the Shroud, National Geographic cover June 1980)

Chapter 6

The times of Jesus

Before going any further, it might help to review for you young people some things about the time Jesus lived.

Rulers:
Tiberius was Roman Emperor, Vitellius was, Legate of Syria and under him Pontius Pilate was Prefect/Procurator of Judea in the south while Herod the Great's son Herod Antipas was Tetrarch *(governor)* of Galilee and Perea. His brother Herod Philip ruled the other outlying areas.

Judea and Samaria:
After King Solomon died, political strife divided the country into Judea in the south, Samaria in the middle, and Galilee in the north. Over time, Samaria became cosmopolitan, and interracially mixed. It treated Judeans as backward. The Samaritans were Hellenized[3] and were not as orthodox as the Judeans. Samaria also had pagan temples. When Jews in Jerusalem rebuilt their temple, Jews in Samaria also built a temple on their Mt. Gerizim. The Judean Jews considered the Samaritan Jews

---

[3] To absorb pagan Greek culture.

as godless heretics. Both had different versions of the Pentateuch[4].

Later, Samaria furnished their foreign overlords with auxiliary troops to help put down rebellions in Judea. The resulting interfaith animosity was apparently like the Protestants and Catholic Christians in Northern Ireland, or the Shiites and the Sunni Muslims in the Middle East.

---

[4] The first five books of the bible.

Jerusalem:

At the time of Jesus, Jerusalem had around 30,000 inhabitants, which would temporarily increase drastically at the time of the Passover to perhaps 100,000. The circumference of the city was believed to be about 3 miles. At the northwest corner of the Temple area *(the large rectangle)*, loomed Fortress Antonia[5] where the Roman troops were quartered, ready to put down any form of revolt in the city.

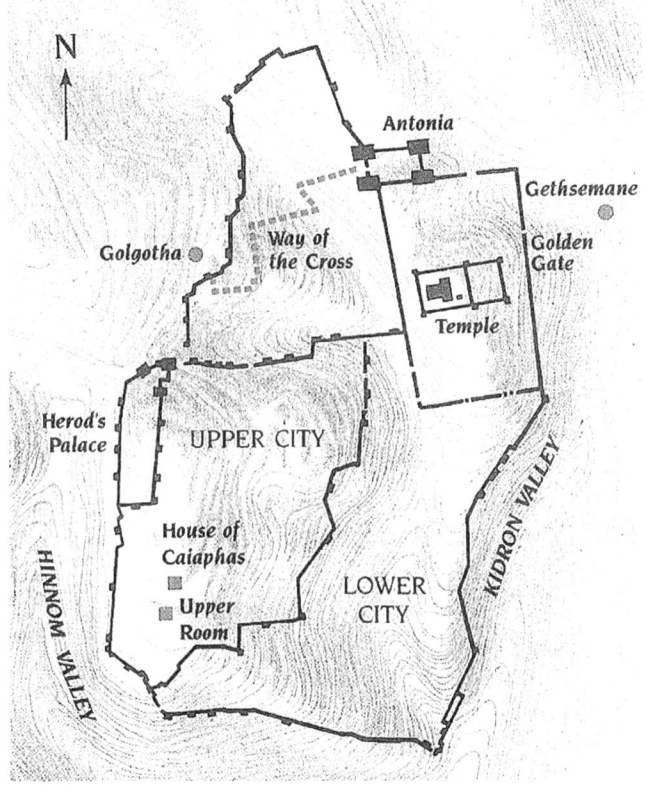

---

[5] Named after Marc Antony by his friend Herod the Great

A biblical aside, is that Herod the Great was the greatest builder in Jewish history and perhaps the most murderous, killing his wives and sons! He had rebuilt the temple Jesus knew, along with the maritime city of Caesarea and fortresses like Masada, Herodium and Antonia. One of his many sons Herod Antipas up in Galilee, had married his brother Philip's wife Herodias whose daughter Salome, danced for him and asked for the head of John the Baptist. The Jews considered Herod the Great more a pagan than a Jew. He was also the king traditionally said to have wanted to kill the infant Jesus.

The Roman Army:
I was in the Marines, where the lowest ranking officer is the **2nd Lieutenant** who leads a **platoon** of forty men. In the Roman Army, the lowest ranking officer was the **Centurion** who led a unit called the **century** composed in theory of a hundred men, but more likely only eighty. Six centuries made up a **cohort** and ten cohorts made up a **legion** of from 5,000 to 6,000 men not counting cavalry and auxiliaries. By comparison, a Marine Division would have upwards of 10,000 men.

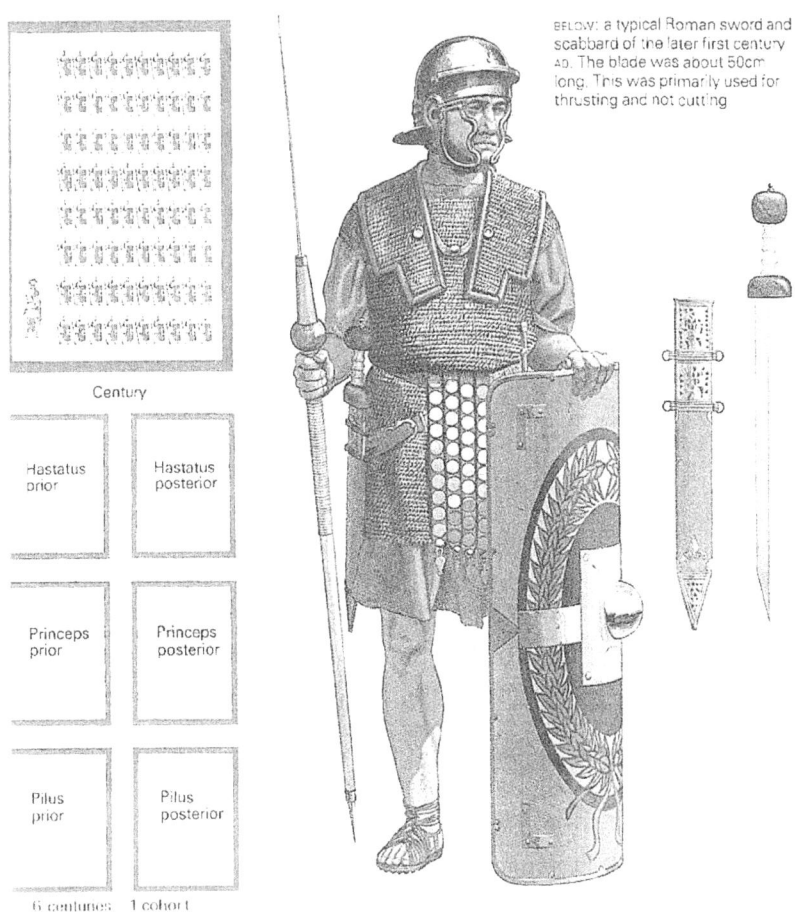

BELOW: a typical Roman sword and scabbard of the later first century AD. The blade was about 50cm long. This was primarily used for thrusting and not cutting.

Jewish social structure:

San-he'-drin: The Supreme Jewish authority in all matters, especially religious. It had seventy one members mainly from the Jewish aristocracy *(Sadducees)*. Herod the Great executed all members who opposed him, and repopulated the Sanhedrin with people who would do his bidding, which in turn was that of pagan Rome. Caiaphas was its head.

Sad'-du-cees: The well-to-do Jewish conservative aristocracy who hung out in Jerusalem and who rejected anything not actually written in the Law of Moses. They didn't believe in an afterlife.

Phar'-i-sees: Were the educated lawyer-like liberal middle class who believed not only in the written Law of Moses, but in addition, the handed down unwritten laws that needed to be continually interpreted and updated *(by them!)* to meet the changing times.

Scribes: Were essentially liberal lawyer-like people who wrote contracts for businesses, marriages, divorces, etc. Usually they were Pharisees

Priests and Levites: Both were of the tribe of Levi and descendants of Moses' brother Aaron. The high Priest and priests were an aristocracy that ran the Temple and religious activities. The Levites were responsible for the logistical activities around the temple, like money changing and maintenance.

Publicans: Rome let Publican Jews like Levi *(Mathew)* collect the taxes. Their salary was whatever they could cheat Rome and/or the people out of. As a result, they were generally considered to be a class of crooks.

Chapter 7

Image evidence on the cloth

In this longer chapter, we'll look at the various wounds and other visual evidence depicted in the cloth.

First of all the man in the Shroud was very tall, roughly 5'11" and weighed perhaps 176 lbs. He was lean, apparently in good shape and somewhere in his 30s or early 40's.

About the head:
The man has definite Semitic features. His hair and beard are also in the Jewish style, certainly not Roman. On the back view of the head can be seen what appears to be a pigtail braiding, another Jewish style of the times *(something no 14th Century forger would know!)*.

The eye/cheekbone to the left appears to be swollen shut. The bridge of his nose also appears to be swollen and the moustache and beard are soaked *(white)* with blood *(nose bleed probably from being punched?)*

"And the men who had him in custody began to mock him and beat him. And they blindfolded him and kept striking his face and asking, "Prophesy, who is it that struck thee"
Luke 22, 63-65

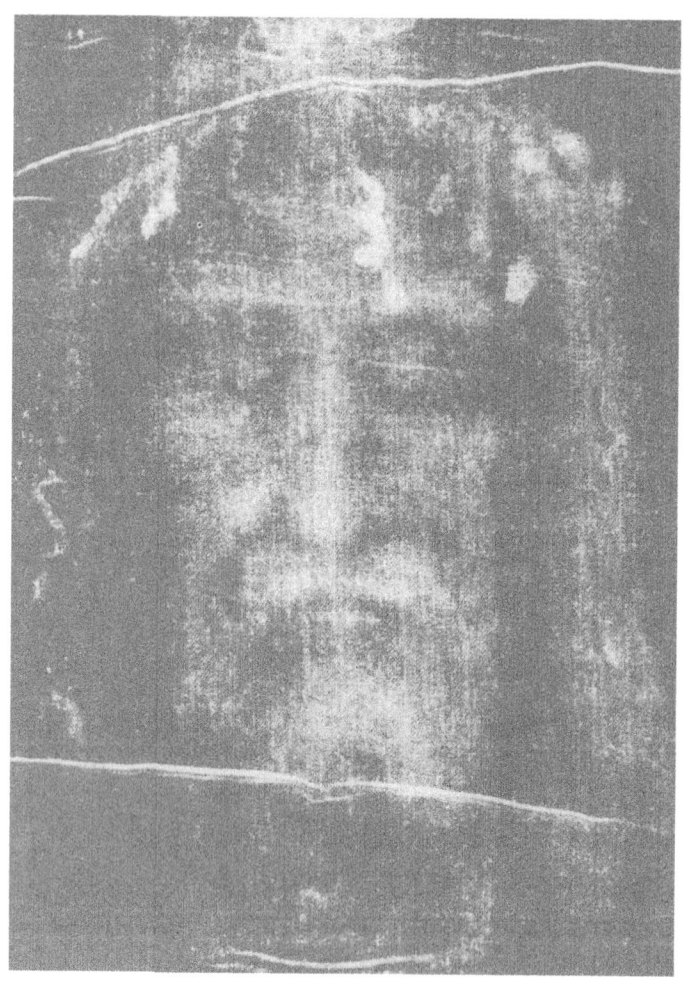

Note the blood trickles *(white)* all over his scalp. Note also the '**3**'-like blood on his brow formed by his furrows.

"Now the soldiers lead him away into the courtyard of the Praetorium, and calling

together the whole cohort, they clothed him in purple, and plaiting a crown of thorns, they put it on him, and began to greet him, "Hail, King of the Jews"

Mark 15, 15-19

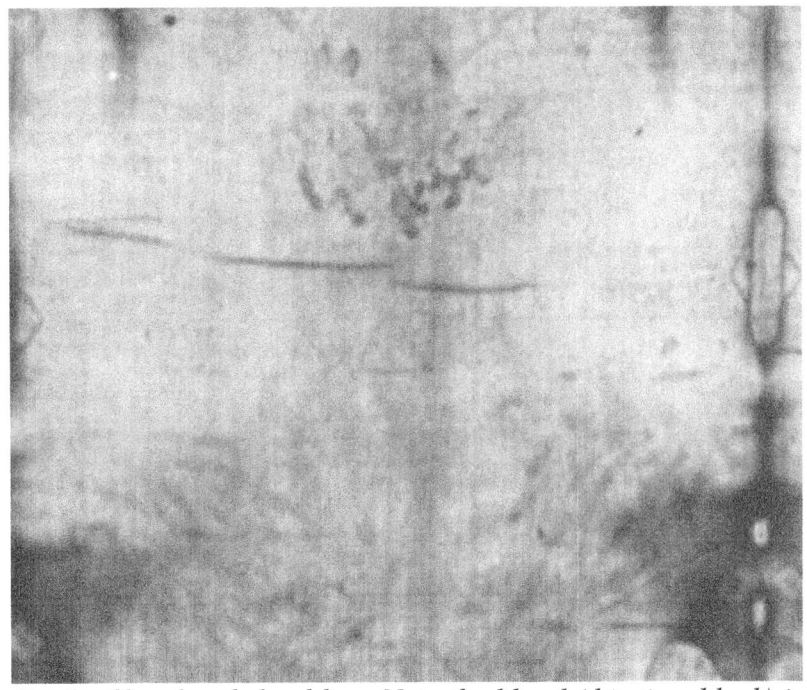

(Back of head and shoulders. Note the blood (this time black) in the scalp hair and braid-like appearance. Note all the scourge marks on the shoulders)

Hands and Chest:

Note the nail wound is in the wrist and that no thumbs are visable! Note the two different blood flow angles on the arms, from blood flowing when trying to stand on the nails, and when hanging limp. Note the belly slightly distended as from asphixia. *(The triangles are repair patches from the fire of 1532).* It is fairly clear, especially from the back, that the man is naked.

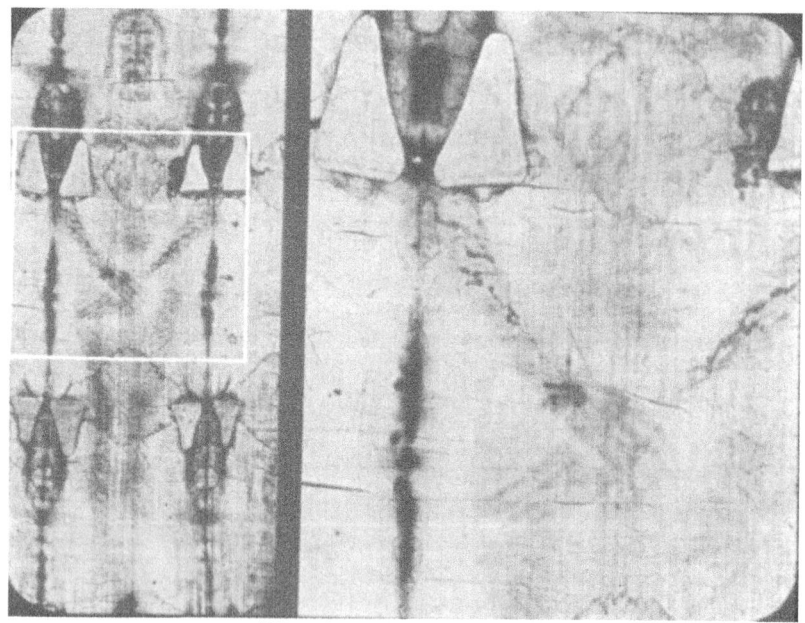

(Hands, arms and chest)

Scourging:

Scourging wasn't normal for a crucifixtion. The whole idea of the Roman punishment was to keep the criminal alive as long as possible, writhing in pain. That's why Jesus died quickly before the other two because he had been greatly weakened from the scourging.

"So Pilate, wishing to satisfy the crowd, released to them Barabbas; but Jesus he scourged and delivered him to be crucified."
Mark 15, 15-19

So, why did Pilate have Jesus scourged? The gospel seem to imply that he didn't find Jesus guilty and wanted to save him. By scourging him, the crowd might be appeased. Pilate also probably didn't want to kill Jesus in order to frustrate Caiaphas and the Sanhedrin whom he hated *(the Sanhedrin had gone behind Pilate's back and complained directly to Rome about his cruel behaviour in Jerusalem. The result was that Pilate was acquiring a bad reputation with the Emperor Tiberius, which made Pilate furious (according to the contemporary Jewish historian Josephus)*.

****

The photo below shows from the back of neck and shoulders down to the waist and butt. Note the angles of the lash marks and the *'dumbell-like'* abrasions. Apparently two men lashed him, one on either side. One can even roughly guess the height of the lashers. Across his waist blood *(black trickles)* pooled as he was being was laid out. The jumble of shapes on either side above the waist are burns and patches from the fire of 1532. The arrow shape in the center of the lower back is a water mark from the fire.

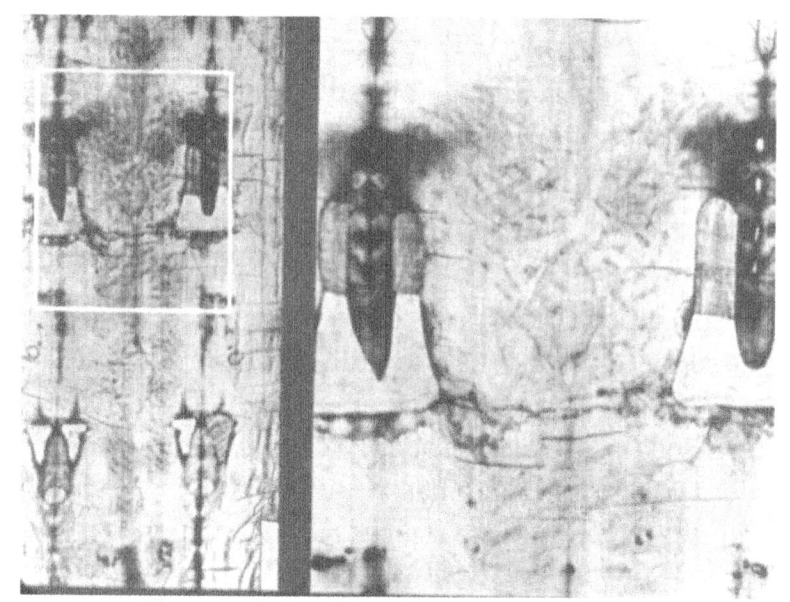

(Scourged shoulders, back, waist and butt)

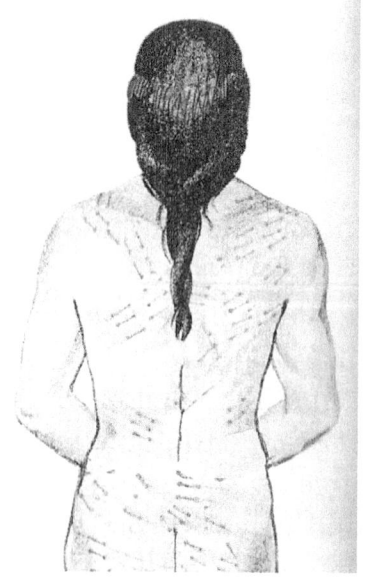

In the photo below note the dumbell-like bloodstains on the Shroud. Next note the Roman flagrum unearthed in the last century from Herculaneum, the city covered by the Vesuvious eruption in 79 AD. Do you mean to tell me that the forgers in 1350± France knew exactly what a Roman flagrum's scourge mark looked like!?

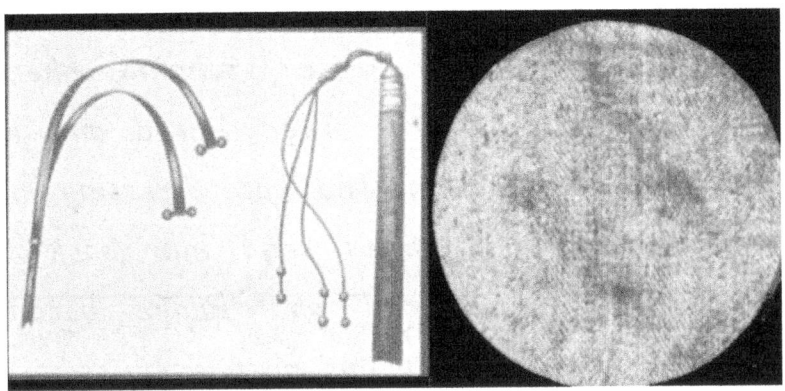

An aside is, that Pilate also wanted to make peace with Herod Antipas. They had been enemies ever since Pilate had quelled a temple riot in 26 AD in which many of Herod's Galileans were killed. Herod also probably didn't want to kill Jesus because Jesus was very popular in Galilee.

On hearing this, Pilate asked if the man was a Galilean. When he learned that Jesus was under Herod's jurisdiction, he sent him to Herod, who was also in Jerusalem at that time. When

Herod saw Jesus, he was greatly pleased, because for a long time he had been wanting to see him. From what he had heard about him, he hoped to see him perform some miracle. He plied him with many questions, but Jesus gave him no answer. The chief priests and the teachers of the law were standing there, vehemently accusing him. Then Herod and his soldiers ridiculed and mocked him. Dressing him in an elegant robe, they sent him back to Pilate. That day Herod and Pilate became friends--before this they had been enemies.

Luke 23

Crucifixion:

There is nothing from Roman times detailing the art of crucifixion. The people of those time knew but apparently saw no point in writing about the cruel practice. In 300AD Emperor Constantine banned the punishment. So from then until 1898 most of what was known as to details came from the gospels that describe Jesus being nailed through the palms of his hands.....at least that's how it was probably badly translated. When I was fifteen, I took Latin. My final exam involved translating Julius Caesar conquering the Helvetians *(Swiss)*. My Latin vocabulary was small, so when I saw *'fruits'*, *'victory'* and *'celebrate'* I creatively came up with,

"Caesar sat down with the Helvetians and had a banquet of fruits to celebrate his victory."

Actually the translation was something more like,

"Caesar beat the hell out of the Helevtians and celebrated the fruits of victory by enslaving the few he hadn't killed!"

I barely got a passing grade for the year.

It's possible some Greek or Latin translation like that ended up with everyone for the past 1,700 years erroneously thinking Jesus was nailed through his palms.

In 1898 when people saw the Shroud photo, they noticed the wounds in the wrist. Immediately anatomists and doctors *(including my Dad's friend Dr. Anthony Sava)* began nailing up cadavers or their arm under tension, and quickly discovered that nails through the palms simply rip out between the fingers.... but a nail through the wrist holds!

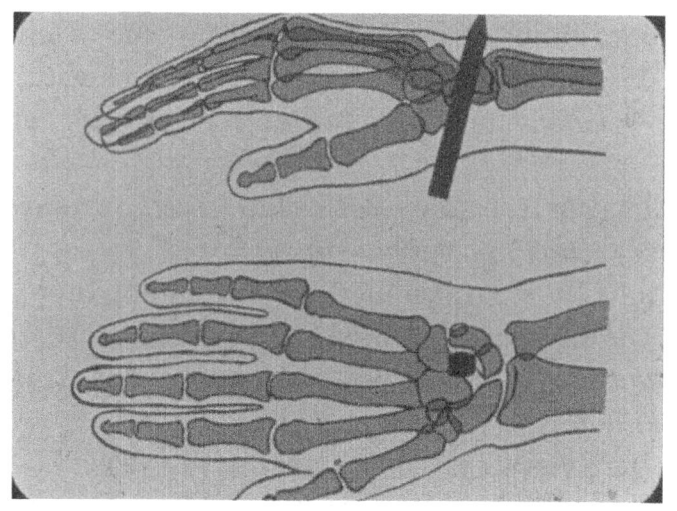

Every painting of the crucifixion ever made, shows the nails in the palms. So why would the forgers in 1350± show something the people didn't believe? How could they possibly know it wouldn't work using the palms?

The doctors discovered something else. When driving a nail through the wrist, the median nerve can be hurt causing the thumb to pull into the palm! Don't try to tell me medieval forgers knew that much anatomy to not show the thumbs!

Note the blood trickles down the forearms from the wrists. The two blood angles tell us at what angle the outstretched arms were when hanging exhausted versus when attempting to stand in order to get a breath!

Next, the medical detectives asked, why a crucified person died? Well, it turns out that hanging limp from outstretched hands caused asphyxiation which in turn causes the chest and abdomen to distend....just like in the Shroud. Did the forgers know this too?! After all, since crucifixions were outlawed in 300AD, they could hardly have been very commonplace in 14th Century France!

The next question was, how did the victims keep from immediately dying? The doctors quickly determined that the criminal could **not** pull himself up with his arms outstretched at 30^0. If a man weighs 176 lbs., then to do a pullup, each arm has to exert a vertical **upward** force of 88 lbs. However, if that man's arms were outstretched at 30^0, then in order to get a vertical upward pull of 88 lbs. per arm, **each** arm would have to pull against its nail at 176 lbs. thus resulting in a combined pull of 2 X 176 or 352 lbs! Nobody except Superman can do that.

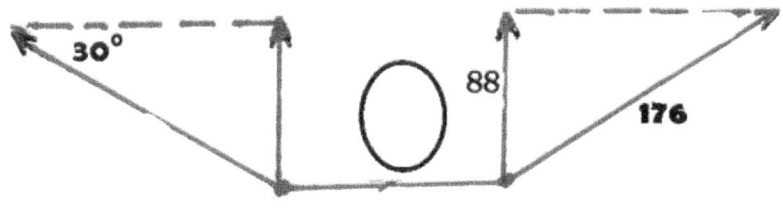

Thus, in order to catch a lifesaving breath, the only possibility was to stand on the nails holding one's feet. Therefore, in order to accelerate death, the executioners simply broke the criminal's legs!

Since it was the day of Preparation, in order to prevent the bodies from remaining on the cross on the Sabbath (Saturday) *(for the Sabbath was a high day), the Jews asked Pilate that their legs might be broken, and that they might be taken away. So the soldiers came and broke the legs of the first, and of the other who had been crucified with him: but when they came to Jesus and saw that he was already dead, they did not break his legs. But one of the soldiers pierced his side with a spear..*

John

The man in the Shroud had his right side pierced by an instrument about the size *(1.75" x .5")* of a Roman lancea blade from Pompeii, found in the Naples Museum.

See the somewhat horizontal, solid dark, flattened, elliptical bean shaped stab wound at the very top of the bloody area. Note all the downward flowing blood that gushes down from it along the side of the repair patch.

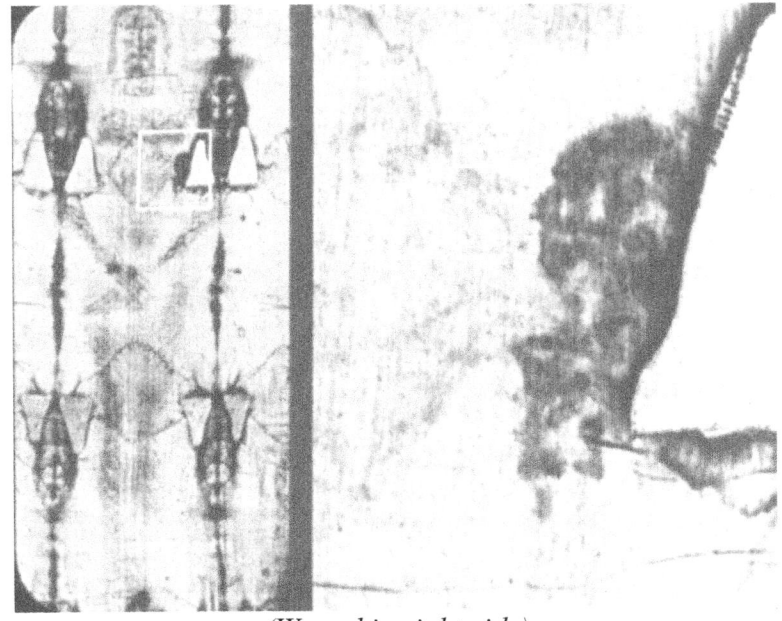

(Wound in right side)

Finally, we come to the feet. The sole of the left foot is bloody, with the main source of blood seeming to originate from what looks like a wound around the center of the ball of the foot. The right foot appears to have been nailed on top of the left. It is also possible however, that the *shroudman* was nailed through his heel bones as was Jehohanan on page 63 below.

Note that the blood flow trickling left from the heel is matched by the same flow on the front view of the feet area.

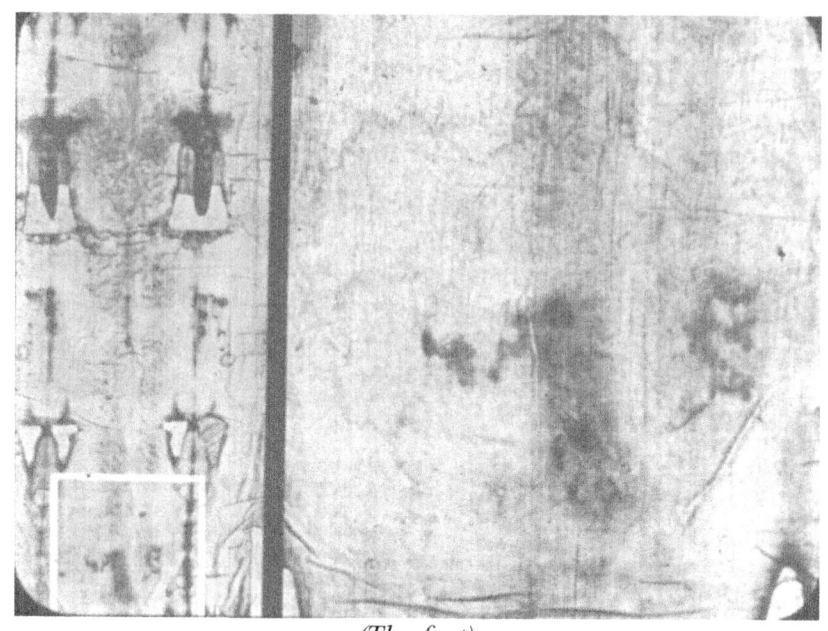
(The feet)

****

Thus it was, that only **after studying the Shroud**, did we learn how crucifixion really worked. In 1968 Israeli archeologists verified this when they found the bones of a crucified Jew named Jehohanan. Below is how the Israelis pictured him. He had been nailed in the wrist area, and had his legs broken. A spike was found protruding from a heel bone, with olive wood still attached to it.

(Jehohanan. Note the bent nail still in the ankle bones)

Notice the man is naked as is the figure in the Shroud. No Christian in the 1300s would accept a relic showing Jesus naked! The Romans on the other hand deliberately executed their victims naked. The fact that it might upset his mother and friends was surely the furthest thing from their minds.

Chapter 8

Burial

Crucified criminals were not given nice burials. They were normally dumped at the city garbage site in a pit. In Jesus' case it was different. He had a secret friend with some political clout.

Now after these things Joseph of Arimathea,...·besought Pilate that he might take away the body of Jesus· And Pilate gave permission· And there also came Nicodemus...·They therefore took the body of Jesus and wrapped it in linen cloths with spices after the **Jewish manner** *of preparing for burial·*
John 19, 38-41

****

Jesus died around 3 PM, and the Sabbath began at sundown, which at the vernal equinox *(March/April)* would be around 6 PM. That gave his friends just under three hours to get him down and buried. But there were real problems:

1) Since the bodies of most crucified people were deliberately dumped in a common pit, Joseph of Arimathea had to go/walk to the praetorium and somehow arrange an audience with Pilate to obtain permission to have the body.

2) Pilate had to get hold of a Centurion and send him out to Golgotha and return to verify Jesus' death.

3) Joseph had to then return back to Golgotha. That all adds up to 4 trips back and forth through crowded streets!

4) Then they had to somehow pry Jesus' body off the cross. Perhaps the soldiers routinely took down the bodies. I don't think it was all that easy.

5) They had to obtain linens and spices.

6) They had to somehow carry the body to a vacant tomb.

All of this between 3 and 6 PM!

I read that ancient Jewish Law forbade washing the corpse of a person who died a violent death e.g. in battle. So Jesus wasn't washed but was left bloody. *(In medieval Europe, the body was usually washed! How did the 1300± forger know to leave the bloody corpse unwashed?)* Jesus followers probably didn't have time anyway. The women obviously planned to return after the Sabbath to do a better job of anointing the corpse with myrrh[6] and aloes and probably trimming and combing his hair and maybe

---

[6] A tree resin used for perfume, incense, and anointing the dead

fingernails etc. before the body started to smell[7]. Also, Jews didn't wrap the body like Egyptians i.e. cocoon like mummy. *(Note, Lazarus hobbled out of his tomb more or less on his own).*

Bodies were frequently left on a limestone shelf in the tomb to decompose, and when only bones remained, these were placed in small stone ossuaries *(as were Jehohanan's back on page 63).*

The shroud man shows indications that the hands and feet might've been tied together, perhaps because of rigor mortis. Also the 3D image hints of possibly a chinstrap.

****

After *Good Friday* can you imagine the utter disappointment and disillusionment of Jesus' followers? They had been convinced he was God sent, the Messiah, and here he was a limp beaten up, bloody corpse, soon to start decomposing and stinking. I feel certain they all must've secretly felt something like,

"I can't believe it, but that's the end of that. We were somehow all led down the garden path. Now we need to go back home to Galilee...back to where we left off before we too are killed. He was the most amazing, wonderful, charismatic, human being we ever met. But in the end he turned out to be a mortal human being and is

---

[7] Jesus said, "Take away the stone." Martha, the sister of the dead man, said to him, "Lord, already there is a stench because he has been dead four days."

now nothing more than a rotting corpse. He sure had us all fooled!"

The tenor of the Gospels for Easter morning is clearly that the women along with Peter and John expected to find nothing other than a cold stiff cadaver, despite Jesus' promise to rise from the dead.

Now on the first day of the week Mary Magdalene came to the tomb early, while it was still dark, and saw that the stone had been taken away from the tomb. So she ran, and went to Simon Peter and the other disciple, the one whom Jesus loved, and said to them, "They have taken the Lord out of the tomb, and we do not know where they have laid him." (notice that she isn't thinking of resurrection, but who stole the corpse!) Peter then came out with the other disciple, and they went toward the tomb. They both ran, but the other disciple outran Peter and reached the tomb first; and stooping to look in, he saw the linen cloths lying there, but he did not go in. Then Simon Peter came, following him, and went into the tomb; he saw the linen cloths lying, and the napkin, which *had been on his head, not lying with the linen cloths but rolled up in a place by itself. Then the other disciple, who reached the tomb first, also went in, and he* **saw and believed**; *(Apparently it was only then that John began believing that Jesus had arisen as he foretold)*

John

Something about the arrangement of the folded shroud caused John to somehow suddenly believe. He saw something, and the lights went on *'and he believed'*. What was it he saw?

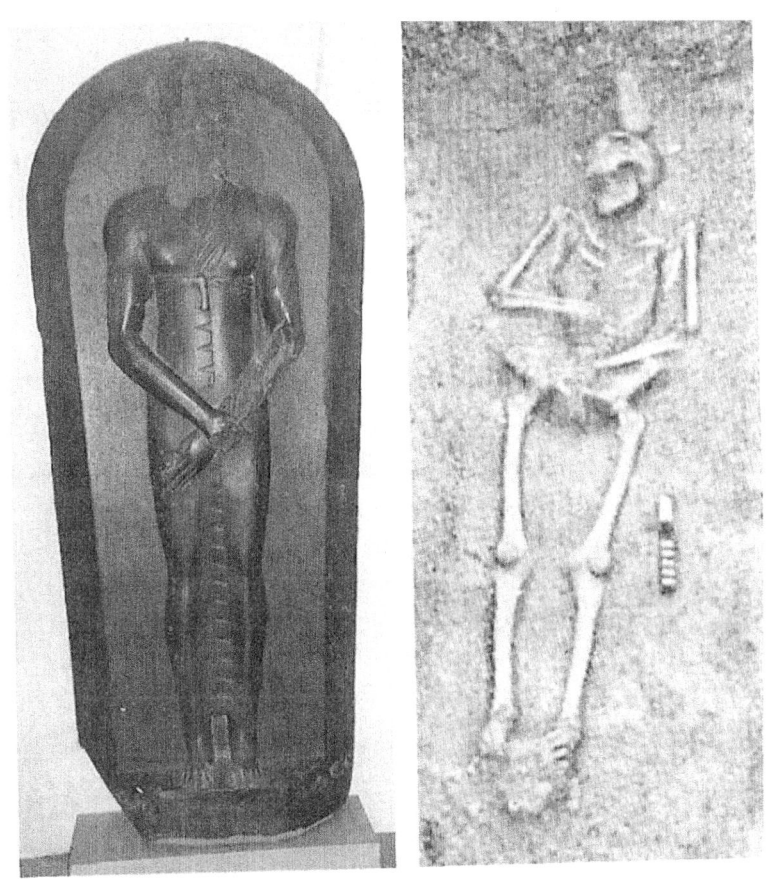

(Body burial layouts from those times)

Chapter 9

Clues from Art

You may remember that in 525 AD the *Mandylion* was discovered hidden in the city gate of Edessa. Prior to that time Christian images of Jesus were of a Roman citizen that is, clean shaven with relatively short hair.

(Jesus the Good Shepherd, note no beard or long hair)

(Other early Christian images of Jesus)

Then starting around 600AD suddenly all subsequent renderings of Jesus show a man remarkably similar to the face in the Shroud. *(remember, the Mandylion was rediscovered in Edessa in 525)*

(Justinian's coin from 629AD)

(Images from 600 to 1300AD. They all look like the Shroud)

(Shroud Jesus by Michael Fuchs of Vienna, 2000)

(Recent artist's version of Jesus; my favorite)

Chapter 10

Probabilities

Some conclusions from the foregoing evidence:
1) It's clearly not a painting, but a **real living** crucified Semitic looking man.
2) The nail wounds were in the wrists. But a 1300 forger to be authentic to every Christian since 300AD, would've nailed through the man's palms! But if he did, the nails would've ripped out if the man were hung, and clearly the man was hung from the blood flow angles on the arms. The forgers would then have to crucify another real Jewish looking man in order to get it right! The palms were not ripped out!
3) Face beaten.
4) Scourged with a whip identical to a Roman flagrum. How likely is it that forgers in 1350± knew what a Roman flagrum looked like?
5) Spear wound in side very similar to a Roman lancea blade.
6) Multiple scalp puncture wounds.
7) With what appears to be a pigtail. Who knew that in 1350± France?
8) Adhering to early Jewish burial custom i.e. unwashed. Who knew that in 1350± France?
9) Corpse removed before decomposing.

10) Containing Middle East pollen and limestone dust, identical to Jerusalem's. How likely is it that 1350± forgers would get Middle Eastern spores and limestone dust in their cloth?

11) The sample was carbon-14 dated around 1300±, but there is certainly the real possibility that the sample could have been contaminated. Until the scientists can get the same carbon-14 dates for the mummy as well as their linen wrapping, the 1988 carbon date results are legitimately suspect.

If it's not Jesus, then it's some poor Semite crucified in 1350± exactly like Jesus.

Bear in mind, that in the Middle Ages, the people of Europe were ignorant, illiterate, superstitious and gullible. Enough *'pieces of the true cross'* were peddled about by returning crusaders and pilgrims to build a housing development! The same goes for nails as well[8]! Why would forgers go to all the trouble of crucifying a real man just to get a cloth with a lot of blood on it? Bear in mind they had no reason to expect a human image to appear. It had never happened before nor for that matter since! All that, just to sell a fake relic? It's possible of

---

[8] See 'the Iron Crown of Lombardy'

course, but considering the times quite a stretch to expect an intelligent person to believe.

Now for some simple Mathematical probabilities[9]:
1) For the sake of argument, let's assume the Romans crucified 1,000,000 men. This means the odds that the man in the Shroud and Jesus could be any one of those million i.e. 1 chance in a million
2) Assume 1/3 of those crucified were Jews/Semetic i.e. 300,000. This means Jesus and the Shroud man have 1 chance in 300,000 of being one of those.
3) Assume ½ had their face pummeled. The odds are now 1 in 150,000.
4) Assume 1 in 10 were scourged with a Roman flagrum. The odds are now 1 in 15,000
5) Assume 1 in 10 had their scalp bloodied *(somehow)*. Odds now 1 in 1,500
6) Assume 1 in 10 were lanced in the right *(not left side, or the stomach nor by a javelin or sword)* 1 in 150
7) Assume 1 in 10 were permitted a *'nice'* burial. The odds are now only 1 in 15!
8) Assume 1 in a 100 was removed from his shroud before corruption set in!!!

---

[9] I was a Math major

Thus anyone with a grammar school education can see that of those million original men crucified, only Jesus *(and the man in the Shroud)* meet all these conditions! All the others are clearly eliminated! And remember, all our numeric assumptions were on the conservative side!

So let's face the facts of the statistics and common sense. The probability is more than 999,999 to 1 that you have been looking at a photographic form of image of the real face of the historical Jesus of Nazareth **or** an unbelievably amazing brilliant 14th century forgery. A forger who went to the extreme of crucifying a tall Jewish looking man. Certainly the forger could not expect any sort of figure to appear on the cloth. No such shrouds ever existed with a full perfect image of any kind! All that would be there on the cloth would be differently located blood smears. So, pig's blood on any old bed sheet would've been just as well believed by the ignorant medieval relic buyer. And how did the forger know to nail him by the wrists if no image would even appear? He would've used the palms as every single Christian up until 1898 *(the Shroud photo)* believed Jesus was nailed! Not only that, how believable is it that the forger scourged him with a real authentic copy of a Roman flagellum, even though archaeologists never came across a real flagellum until excavating Herculaneum in the 19th century! That he then went to all the trouble of using a non-European shaped shroud whose weave was relatively uncommon in 14th century Europe and placed the head where Europeans expected his feet? Also a cloth bearing Middle Eastern spores that medieval people didn't even yet know existed, and were anyway impossible for them to even see, and limestone dust from the region of Israel!

Let's face it, believing in such a brilliant 14th century forger is far harder to swallow, than that Jesus's actual shroud exists today in Turin!

Author John Walsh wrote in his book, *"its either one of the most ingenious and unbelievable products of the human mind and hand*

or

the most awesome and instructive relic of Jesus Christ in existence, imprinted with a 2000 year old image of Him as he lay in death."

This cloth is not some trick, not some clever painting, not some kind of optical illusion, not some fake, but <u>in all likelihood</u> the real, **actual image** of the dead Jesus, whom you grandchildren and I **believe** to be the Messiah, the Son of God!!!

****

Oh, and if you are wondering how such a unique perfect negative image occurred, there have been many theories, but none of them too believable. In other words, nobody knows!

Thus anyone with a grammar school education can see that of those million original men crucified, <u>only Jesus *(and the man in the Shroud)*</u> meet all these conditions! All the others are clearly eliminated! And remember, all our numeric assumptions were on the conservative side!

So let's face the facts of the statistics and common sense. The probability is more than 999,999 to 1 that you have been looking at a photographic form of image of the real face of the historical Jesus of Nazareth **_or_** an unbelievably amazing brilliant 14th century forgery. A forger who went to the extreme of crucifying a tall Jewish looking man. Certainly the forger could not expect any sort of figure to appear on the cloth. No such shrouds ever existed with a full perfect image of any kind! All that would be there on the cloth would be differently located blood smears. So, pig's blood on any old bed sheet would've been just as well believed by the ignorant medieval relic buyer. And how did the forger know to nail him by the wrists if no image would even appear? He would've used the palms as every single Christian up until 1898 *(the Shroud photo)* believed Jesus was nailed! Not only that, how believable is it that the forger scourged him with a real authentic copy of a Roman flagellum, even though archaeologists never came across a real flagellum until excavating Herculaneum in the 19th century! That he then went to all the trouble of using a non-European shaped shroud whose weave was relatively uncommon in 14th century Europe and placed the head where Europeans expected his feet? Also a cloth bearing Middle Eastern spores that medieval people didn't even yet know existed, and were anyway impossible for them to even see, and limestone dust from the region of Israel!

Let's face it, believing in such a brilliant 14th century forger is far harder to swallow, than that Jesus's actual shroud exists today in Turin!

Author John Walsh wrote in his book, *"its either one of the most ingenious and unbelievable products of the human mind and hand*
or
the most awesome and instructive relic of Jesus Christ in existence, imprinted with a 2000 year old image of Him as he lay in death."

This cloth is not some trick, not some clever painting, not some kind of optical illusion, not some fake, but in all likelihood the real, **actual image** of the dead Jesus, whom you grandchildren and I **believe** to be the Messiah, the Son of God!!!

****

Oh, and if you are wondering how such a unique perfect negative image occurred, there have been many theories, but none of them too believable. In other words, nobody knows!

"....it is either one of the most ingenious, most unbelievable products of the human mind and hand on record....or....the most awesome and instructive relic of Jesus Christ in existence...."
writer John Walsh

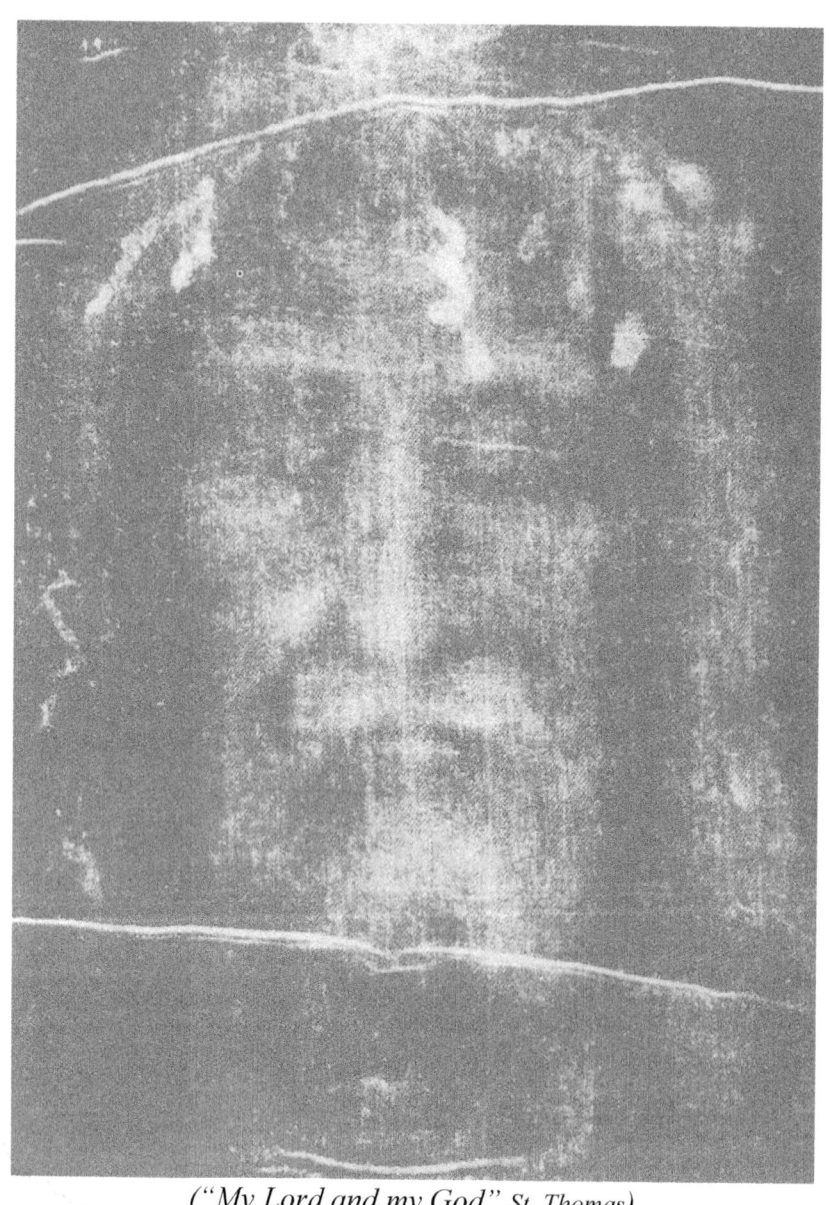

("My Lord and my God" St. Thomas)

The End

(If you are interested in reading a well written book on the subject, read *The Blood and the Shroud* by Ian Wilson)

Made in the USA
Monee, IL
04 April 2021